Emerging Through the Shadows

Emerging Through the Shadows

THE JOURNEY OF A WRITER

poetry & musings

A. N. TIPTON

Book Cover by A.N. Tipton

Edited by Janna Lopez

ISBN: 979-8-9917857-0-9

1st Edition 2024

Dedication

This is to all writers who have the bravery to fall in love with their words thus spreading that love to all their readers.

Contents

Introduction

This human journey is full of complexities, experiences, varying perceptions, and riotous emotions. Like many during the pandemic, I found myself swept into a current of confusion, fear, growth and increased creativity. It felt as if I, along with the world, were thrown into this forced vortex of change and growth. This brought forth the opportunity to turn to my words and deepen my journey as a w riter.

This book is a collection of poems and musings from my journey as a writer unearthed during the pandemic, up until 2023. Writing has always been a comfort for me. It's a way to release and express that which lives under my skin. During the time of global strife, in particular, I found myself on a journey of transformation and exploration as I connected to deeper aspects of myself through words. I traversed through a world which included both shadow and light.

Here's the thing: We are human. And yet, we are divine beings. I searched for balance and peace during a time when fear, change, and chaos descended upon the planet. I was forced to be still and alone with myself. I was invited to work with parts of my shadow, and at the same time, deepen the relationship with my spirituality. This book has aspects of uncomfortable darkness, of divinity, of healing, of grief, of trauma, and a little fun.

Many of the poems are streams of consciousness, unedited, and raw. Whether born from a prompt, a need to expel darkness, or express the light, they are a part of my truth; a kaleidoscope of aspects of myself unfolding through words. Some of the poems are merely a birth of creativity. Putting words out into the world takes courage. Sharing truth is an extremely vulnerable act. However, there is power in vulnerability.

Interspersed in these pages are musings and essays from my blog, *The Journey of a Writer* series. Here is where I explored the evolution of my relationship with words.

I now offer these words to the world. To you. As I release them, my hope, my silent prayer, is that at least one person will relate, or maybe heal a little, or receive simple pleasure from the words. This offering is also given to myself as a gift of bravery. I am humbled. I am in deep gratitude. I am absolutely terrified.

With all the love in my heart.

Enjoy.

Is This the Power of Our Words?

the wave of creation comes as inspiration

The inspiration hits,
out of the blue.
Words invade my head,
like an insistent toddler.
Do I stop what I'm doing to write it down?
Yes. Yes, I do.
I whip out my phone
and open the notes app,
just to get words down.
Choosing to listen to this invitation of inspiration,
I open up myself, calm my mind and surrender.
The wave of creation flows in and through my crown,
collecting pieces inside
that need to be expressed and released.
The first words come,
then they inspire the next,

and the next,
until I fall into a cadence,
into a sensual fluidity of textures and slopes.
Until I can taste sorrow,
and smell elation,
and hear octaves
in forms of density and light.
Can one really describe with words,
the feeling of creation?
Writers try.
All the time.
My Muse does pirouettes
on my shoulder,
while my Inner Critic pouts,
her arms and legs crossed.
I turn away and feel for that thread,
the one that leads towards somewhere magical.
This time I'm surprised by the words spilling out.
They are dark and angst.
They shiver like fear and twist
into a week's worth of unsettled feelings.
And yet, I surrender.
I open up, soften–
a mother comforting her newborn.
I give those parts of myself a voice,
the ones trapped in survival,
flight or fight,
uncertainty and sorrow.
They unravel, a spool,
once tightly wound
but now loose and languid.
I'm grateful,

because words inform
of what festered,
like cancer,
crouched in dark, hidden corners.
They merge into a sacred offering,
one of pain,
transmuted and reimagined into form.
The wave of creation
slows to a trickle
then stills altogether.
I acknowledge
what words want me to know.
A truth of me at that moment.
Maybe the truth of me will be different the next moment,
and the moment after that.
A vine, reaching for light,
crawling up cracked mortars of my mind.
Or perhaps my heart.
Until warm honey settles deep into my bones like liquid gold,
illuminating the cells of my body(s).
My mind feels cleansed,
my body relaxed and my spirit elevated.
I feel lighter,
expelling what holds me back,
through the form of words.
A small smile graces my face,
for my Muse is kneeling next to the Inner Critic,
enveloping her in a warm hug.
And the three of us settle into
this new truth of me.
And I wonder...
Is *this* the power of words?

Are we messengers,
scribing realities into being,
spreading results of flowing creation
onto pages?
Can our words heal us, soothe us, incite us?
Do we choose the words,
or do words choose us?
What secrets do our words hold,
even from ourselves?
What do they have to tell us?
And I realize,
I am here
to listen.

The Journey of a Writer
Musings

Confessions of a Closet Writer

I have a confession. I am a closet writer. I'm an aspiring author. I have multiple half finished novels in my proverbial drawer, and two complete first draft manuscripts. I write poems. I write blog posts that I hesitate to put my name on, and I journal.

I've belonged to writing groups, critique groups, gone to endless writing workshops and conferences, stalked my favorite authors, and read countless books on how to write. I create what a writer should be, should do, or should write, in my head. I hold to a rigid, tangled mess of beliefs that validate an Inner Critic that tells me I should keep words to myself.

Hidden. Secret.

All the while, the closet writer within wants to burst free and blaze into the light.

Why do I hold myself back? Why does any writer? Over the years, I've repeatedly asked myself these questions. The Inner Critic hammers me with self-deluded questions, and inserts its insidious beliefs. *What if I'm not good enough? What business do I have writing? What if people don't like it? What makes what I have to say so important? Oh God, what if my relatives read my writing? That would make for an interesting holiday dinner...*

As a writer, my words are my guts. The inner-workings of a fractured psyche, a peak behind the curtain. My characters represent the flawed, crystal facets of the little broken pieces of me. My 'conflicts' are an expression of my perceived traumas and insecurities. My words are clues to emotions stored deep within hidden depths. To release my words into the world makes me vulnerable. Oh, so vulnerable.

I'd be seen. My words and I splayed out onto a proverbial cross, a crucifixion of my soul. Not only would my expression allow the masses to pick and prod through the skeletal remains of my hidden depths, but then I might have to take a deeper look. At myself. At the hidden depths that I've camouflaged so well, and had neatly-wrapped into excuses, rewrites, edits, and the voice of my Inner Critic. Which brings me to the biggest predator of all, the one that stalks relentlessly:

Fear.

Fear is the great deceiver, controller of the masses, stunter of growth, depressor of creativity, the adversary, the chaotic voices and thoughts, and creator of viral beliefs. I let fear control me, inform me, hold me back from stepping out of my closet, my comfort zone. Is it fear of seeing myself? Of holding myself accountable? Of allowing myself to be vulnerable?

When I truly think about it, writing has always been a sanctuary. From the very first diary I kept, I expressed a barrage of words that were kept tightly-contained within my little body. Writing was a gift. All the things I wasn't allowed to say, express, or that weren't safe to share, went behind that unicorn in the form of words.

The act of writing is powerful. Words are a gateway into our pain, our hopes, our beliefs, our histories, our deep sovereignty, our truth. Words create worlds, characters, retell age-old stories, teach and inform. Words brought me through tough times, gave hope, became my friend, taught me about who I want to be, and what kind of world I want to create. I've clung to the words of others like a lifeline. I've poured my words of pain and joy onto the page. The silent therapist, great observer, the quiet listener.

Perhaps the admission, through writing this, is a first step to come out of the closet. A bare foot poking out of the darkness of a jarred door, into a lighted hallway. Perhaps there are others out there, too, who consider themselves closet writers. Others who also hold words tight, suppress their power, behind closed doors for fear of the light or of being seen.

So here I am. Taking this step. Maybe it will be the first and only step. Or maybe, just maybe, this will be the first of many steps, one that creates a path of empowered words. Maybe I'll do this alone. Or maybe, just maybe, others will share their words, too, and come out of their closets beside mine.

Imposter Syndrome

I feel it creep in,
sneak behind,
slither around
my psyche
as feelings of
inadequacy

I want to throw
the computer,
erase my words,
dump the work
into a black hole
of the trash folder

What are these words
that are trying
to sound good,
be clever,
creativity distilled
in whole-hearted
dismay

I am an imposter
the syndrome is real
under false beliefs
of grandiose ideals
to be whittled down
to nothingness and
hypocrisy

I wonder what others
see, hear, feel
with my words
rattling in their heads
like brittle bones
ready to break

Do they think too...
that I am an imposter?

Gaia the Healer
Poems

Island

I'm an island,
surrounded
by saltine waves,
sucking me,
towards an end
of the world,
a sinking sphere
of liquid fire,
only to fade
into fields
of empty stars.

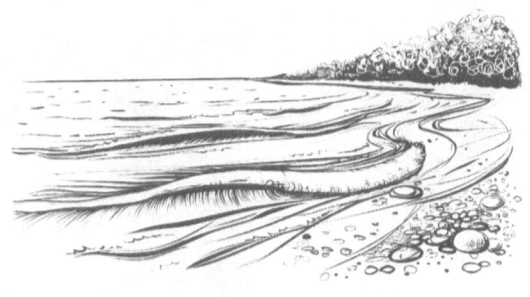

Arbor Dreams

Crossing a line
into the sublime,
into nowhere and everywhere
without a care.

Trees,
they spoke to me,
in soft whispers
carried on the breeze.

Sacred promises, timeworn truths,
stored in roots,
buried through time,
in fertile ground,
waiting, waiting.

The ancient giants
sing through their leaves.
Swaying, unfurling, shading,
a never-ending song of creation.

Of never and always,
timeless eternity.
Cycles of civilizations rise,
fall,
forgotten,
rewritten,
changed,
but always the same.

Spark of humanity,
the eternal soul,
an indestructible spark of love.
Mother Gaia spinning,
dancing in her universe
as life dips and swirls
in reverence of undiluted memories.

Bathing in the forest's breath,
connecting to damp soil
as nature's symphony
echoes in weighted silence.

Never to be silenced,
Always to endure,
in realities of
our heart-centered beauty,
as the arbor's dream
their never-ending dreams.

Elements

Water,
flows like magic
down down down
into lips of
a tongue
tender with words
and silky caresses
beckoning from the
inside out
rushing like blood
a river of life
carving into walls
of our parched hearts

Earth,
nurtures like mother
down down down
into Gaia's heart center
pulsing
drums and fire
soaking in
light rays of
prisms
and quartz dreams
embracing us in
her tree-like limbs

Air,
breathes like life
down down down
into currents
shifting
timelines
and paradigms
singing life
into our lungs
and our words
speaking power and truth
into being

Fire,
cleanses like pain
down down down
into a white hot
golden center of
passionate fervor
ever-burning
love
divine flames
entwined lovers
in an age-old
dance

Elements,
aspects of creation
chaos and birth
bringing alchemy
building this reality
with soothing tears
an uplift of song
of green growing things
existing in fits
of righteous rage
explosion of particles
into this thing called life

Communion

have you ever stood
in weighted silence
surrounded by trees?
do you ever feel awed
by these ancient, majestic beings?

do you give gratitude
to the lungs of Mother Gaia,
knowing that without
our limbed brethren,
we could not breathe freely?

do you hear
their never-ending song?
do you feel their pain
at our lack
of reverence?

Maybe, as I,
you've learned
to turn off the ability
to commune with them

because it's painful to hear
the trees' mournful songs.

they sing of times lost,
peace gone
and mass genocide
upon their species.

we pretend not to know,
us humans,
because then
we have to
acknowledge
shared pain.

for what we do to earth,
we do to ourselves.
we've been taught
we are separate
and we take on
this belief
as true.

lost,
they sing
lost into obscurity,
as are you,
they sing,
remember us.

I lay my cheek
against the bark,
rough, but alive.
I know,

my soul whispers back
in a universal language
we all speak,
even when
we have forgotten.

I take and give comfort
to the wise ones,
our exchange silent,
yet powerful.
honoring,
resting,
breathing,
unto this communion.

knowing
the pain exists,
and yet,
for this eternal moment,
we are one.

Moon Dreams

in the dreamscape
the midnight hour coalesces
as her lunar celestial body presides
with silvery rays of moonbeams

her fullness calls out to me tonight
the pull of her essence
her glowing orb of luminescence
shines upon all sacred spaces

she cleanses my soul
my pain
and gravitates all that is needed
into my path

night flowers
unfurl upon her presence
safe in dark spaces
in her magical glow

her mystery haunts
as I walk through the moonlit garden

seducing me with a lure
of her beauty

she amuses me
never accuses me
or loses me
always loves me

for there is a kind of light
breaking through shadows
the starry night invokes
with her soft illumination

and when my eyes open
to another dreamscape of reality
her soothing song still resides
within my very soul

as I walk this Earth
footsteps pressing against Gaia's skin
tides of her lunar melody
flow forever within my life's blood

The Ocean and Me

Once upon a rainy, dreary day,
the Ocean's song answered my call
with waves of compassion
and infinite wisdom.

Her white crests flatten
and kiss my toes, washing me clean.
I drop down into my grateful heart,
and send back waves of love and gratitude.

And for a moment we become one,
the Ocean and me,
to exist in forever now,
communing as Mother Gaia intended.

Salty winds smooth over my eye lashes,
her gentle exhalations
inviting to behold
the sight of a new day.

We caused a shift,
the Ocean and me,

one that reverberated throughout my very soul,
grounding me to the tunes of the Earth.

And so, I take her invitation,
as waves sing their
crashing crescendo behind me,
like an avenging Goddess.

With eyes anew, the worldview changed,
morphing into endless possibilities
promises and truths of
our inherent divine sovereignty.

The Ocean whispers to me,
of things forgotten,
tales of an untold past, present and future,
readying my soul for remembrance.

For it is time, she sighs,
time to awaken,
time to shine your inner flame
and remember your eternal power.

For we are made of the same
as stardust, existing in the
continuous cycle of the cosmos,
the Ocean and me.

Slumbering Giant

Slumbering giant,
towering giant,
standing tall, a proud parent
in your kingdom of green.

Years pass by,
rings hidden in your timber,
marking the rise
and fall of the sun.

Ancient and regal,
you stand alone,
and yet you're rooted deep,
connected to earth

A hidden underground network
roots of arbors
that look up to you,
a sea of rolling treetops.

You are their protector.

Even from a distance away,
I feel your noble presence,
emanating in the clearing,
blanketing everything that surrounds you.

I close my eyes,
accepting your peace,
and deep, silent wisdom
that resonates in my soul.

You are alive,
more alive than any of us,
swaying in the gentle breeze,
ever watchful and resilient.

We connect,
a moment of breath,
for you are the lungs of Gaia,
making it possible for mine to work.

I honor you.

We are the same, in oneness,
your majestic pillar of eons
vibrating at a coherent tone of conversation,
that needs no words.

Because in that moment of awe,
I feel you.
I feel your infinite presence,
I feel your abiding peace,

I feel your ancient wisdom,
I feel your nobility

and evergreen of acceptance.
I feel your love.

I find it incomprehensibly,
impossible to ignore you,
shining like a quiet beacon,
a brave sentinel of cycles past.

Do you feel my deepening gratitude?

Slumbering giant,
towering giant.

The Breath of the Ocean

The beach allows my soul to breathe.

Sand under the woven blanket
molds to the dips
and curves of my body,
warming me from the bottom.

I feel earth's energy
thrum against my palms,
almost like resistance a magnet gives,
vibrating like an invisible motor.

She soothes me, the Earth.

I pull salty pieces of hair
out of my mouth,
and lean my face into a briny breeze,
accompanied by the sun's brilliant rays.

I pull in golden radiance
through my pores,

my skin hungers for warmth
to infuse my weary soul.

Inhale
Exhale
Repeat

The ocean's song
quietly roars my muscles
into languid
conduits of soothing.

She gently rocks tensions away, the Ocean.

With swishes,
and crashing waves,
and deepening thrum with her symphony
in concert with Earth and Sky.

Their sacred triad.

I sit in their vortex,
allowing alignment of my triad,
(body, mind and spirit)
to the same song,
the octaves
eternal and primordial.

Oneness
Inhale
Openness
Exhale
I Surrender
Repeat

Into folds of in-between and nothingness,
I ride waves of color,
iridescent streams of light shows,
carrying me in timeless wonder.

I land softly unto waking knowing,
shadows of birds temporarily tattoo my skin,
emblems of freedom with unapologetic abandon.

Eyelids lift to the glittering horizon,
crystal visions burst with clarity
and quiet power.

Emerging
Weaving
Remembering

My weary soul is refreshed,
oxygen infused veins
pulsate exquisite joy.

I lay in silent awe,
aside the Ocean's breath.

The beach allows my soul to breathe.

The Journey of a Writer
Musings

Am I a Writer or Not?

I used to call myself an 'aspiring author.' That was when I had an unhealthy relationship with my Inner Critic. When I allowed insecurities and fears of being seen to dictate creativity. My Inner Critic encouraged me to put words in a box, and hold them close with a belief that being vulnerable, and seen, weren't safe.

So, in the past I *aspired* to write. But I still wrote, because writing was breathing for my soul. The words might have been placed in a box, but they begged to escape my head, my fingers, my heart. Characters cried out for recognition. Scenes would replay in my mind until I was forced to sink into the feeling, textures, emotions and fluidity. And when I called myself an aspiring author, I'd ignore the hollow feeling in the pit of my stomach caused by the declaration.

I was in the closet. Hiding, holding on to pointless shame, and the belief that I wasn't good enough. The term 'Aspiring Author' sometimes paralleled 'Closet Writer.'

Then one day, I came across an article, and for the life of me I cannot remember where or who wrote it, but it called out the words *Aspiring Author*. It brought up the question, "Do you *aspire* to be an author, or *are* you an author?"

I sat with the question for a long time. I realized that I was holding myself back, taking baby steps, showing my work to a small number of people. I would write and rewrite the same piece, until all the color leaked out, and the richness of the process fell flat. The writing was never good enough, or polished enough, or the plot wasn't developed enough. Any excuse or justification was acceptable, and perfectionism became a form of procrastination and self-sabotage.

My Inner Critic sat on my shoulder, with devil horns and silky lies, and whispered into my ear words of doubt and criticism. This led me to compare my unpublished work, to that of the work of my published, favorite authors. I was comparing my worst to their best. Because *that's* a healthy benchmark, right? *Thank you, Inner Critic.*

Fast forward to the present: I now call myself a *Writer*. Perhaps some may point out the difference between a *writer* and an *author*, and that's okay. The thing is, I've been on a journey. A journey of self-exploration, acceptance, and growth as a writer. I like how *Writer* sounds to my ears. I like how *Author* feels in my solar plexus.

I decided to push my Inner Critic off my shoulder, silence the constant whispering, and embrace *my* words, my freedom. Yeah, in the spirit of transparency, quieting my Inner Critic is a constant battle. She can be a contentious *b!#@h* sometimes. And yet, the more I silence her, the easier it gets.

So here I am.

Authoring, not aspiring.

And as always, my journey as a writer continues.

Word by Word

Letters spill onto the page like magic,
ink leaking worded images through
seamless strokes of the pen.

Bursts of primary colors
come alive through adjectives and verbs,
evoking emotional responses from their avid audience.

Wordy descriptions lend
to details of twists and turns
of epic storytelling.

Beneath artistic sentences,
truth emerges, touching souls
whose paragraphs enter their eyes.

They fall into other worlds,
hypnotized by adventure, heartbreak, wins, and wars,
where the pen is mightier than the sword.

For words create realities,
mold civilizations, and people's minds.
For praise be to the storytellers!

Whose purpose is to lead, lift,
taint, and lure others to provocative ideas,
forever altering inner landscapes,

One mind at a time.
Word by word.
Letter by letter.

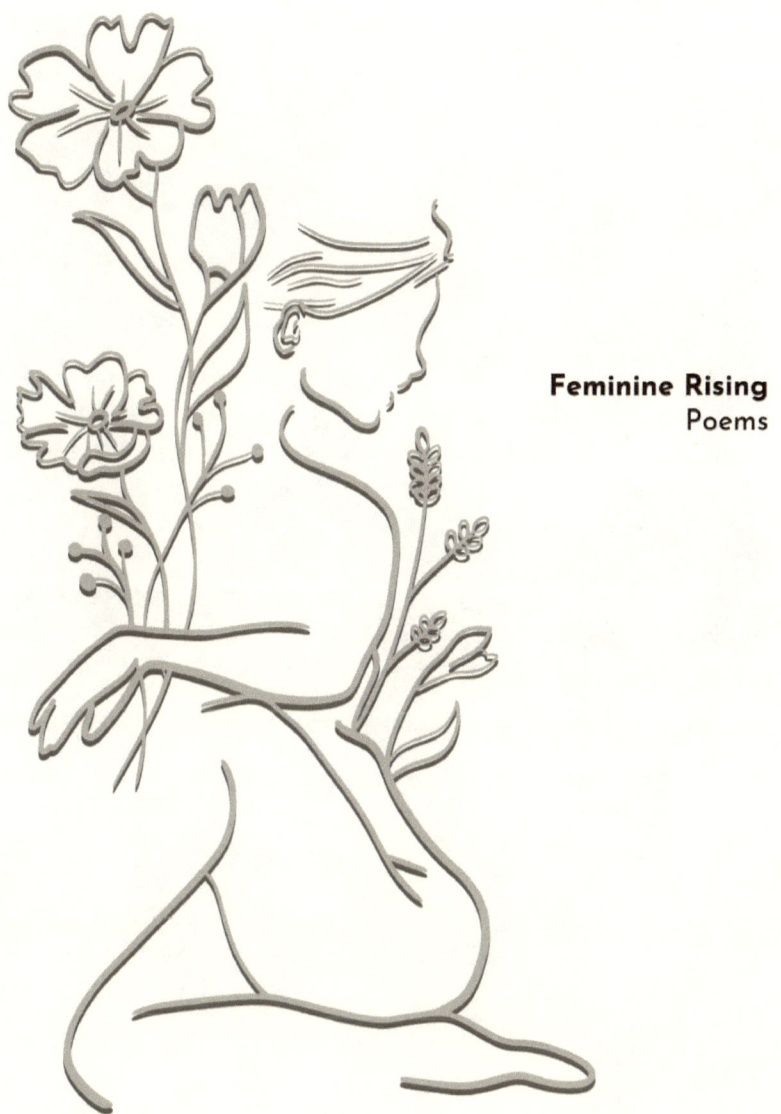

Feminine Rising
Poems

Absence

I am the black womb,
point of creation,
Great Mother
of all.
From my void
became thought,
which became a spark
and then
became.
Into being.

In the absence,
a spark of light
illuminated the nothingness,
dark,
beautiful,
safe,
warm,
until light rays
bounced into
prisms of realities.

I am the black womb
from which
your divinity shines,
created
by purity
of the eternal,
to give life.

A primordial birthing.
Giver of life.
For which
absence breeds,
within
place of power.

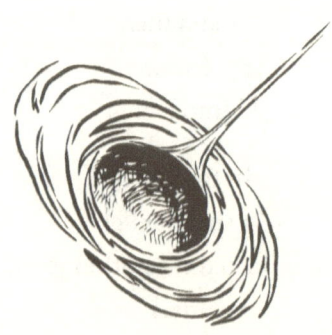

Arise

She folds into herself,
shell of protection,
saving her from the
lashing of the soul.

No more,
she cries in despair,
rock bottom,
tears falling onto barren land.

Broken,
into unrecognizable pieces
unable to see
a way out.

But,
she is never alone,
for her divinity
shines eternal.

Remember,
the small ember whispers
that lives
in her sacred heart.

A tiny pinprick
of light,
piercing darkness,
she opens her eyes.

To a new
path of existence
born of pain and
suffering.

For whom other,
than those who've
been tempered by fire,
to lead us into a new world.

Awakened
to her silent power,
undefeatable,
claiming divinity within.

Arise,
and fear no more,
for when all is lost,
all is regained.

A Work In Progress

The beauty within
was turned to sin
by fear and greed
and undeniable need.

She locked her heart away
taking her part in the play
acting out her scripted scene
all the while being unseen.

Her soul cried out loud
tired of being under a shroud
of being repressed
and of feeling less.

Until she saw in his eyes
what he was unable to disguise
the truth of her allure
as passion began to stir.

Deep from an unforgiving womb
expanding in room

for all the love in her soul
making her whole.

Birth

birth
painful
beautiful
love abounds
into a tiny bundle
of wrinkled skin
and howls of
discontentment
until they hear
their mother's voice.

birth can be painful
is painful
for all involved
but pain
is the catalyst
of becoming
something new.

I was cheated
of his birth

as they cut him
out of me
clinical
necessary
and I wonder

would our bond
be different
if I felt pain
another way?
does it matter?
did I really give birth
or just gestate
another being
into beingness?

Priestess

Welcome
to
the Priestess-hood
sister mine we're
understood.
Shining bright.

Where wisdom
abounds
with sacred sounds
activate healing
Her
She
Us
All

Initiated into
her
divine light,
accepting
the
mantle bright.
Divine sovereignty

Stars for eyes
seeing through
lies
activate clearing
Her
She
Us
All

Connecting
to
paradigm
shifting
into
this new timeline.
Anchoring light.

Our voices harmonize
Elevating ancient
reprise
activate love
Her
She
Us
All

She Is a Woman

She is a woman
with all her flaws
and all her beauty

She walks the earth
with demons behind
and angels ahead

She's resilient
because it's in her DNA and
because she's had no other choice

She is a woman
creator of lives
with a warrior's heart

She is a woman who refuses
to give into societal shame
born of their separation

She is a woman
with all her trauma
and with all her love

And she rises
with her sisters and
for her sisters

She stands tall
unafraid of her feminine power
shining sovereignty for all

She is chanting,
invoking divine healing and balance
for all, within her thrall

She is a woman
and the time is now
to embrace all the beauty within

She Remembers

She allows tears to fall
into the earth
cleansing drops of magic
transforming, transmuting
releasing in a holy bath.

The earth reaches up
holding her in the
Great Mother's arms
allowing space.

And she remembers
connection that was forgotten
in creation
of daily life.

She remembers
that she is divine,
sacred,
powerful.

She remembers
repressed truths
that were forced to hide.
She remembers.

More tears fall
but this time of joy
and relief,
of oneness.

She lays her body
on fertile land
staring at clear
blue skies

where earth and sky meet
where as above, so below,
where everything aligns
in perfect harmony.

And she rests
in perfect connection,
gratitude in her heart
meets the gratitude

in the Great Mother's
in perfect understanding.
Thank you, Mother Goddess.
So be it and so it is.

She Rises

the heart of the womb
blazes from righteous love
the divine feminine

repressed, oppressed, pushed down
where lies became the narrative
until she flows beneath our skin

like a silent river
nourishing her sisters quietly
forever immortal in her love

perceived weakness belies
her iron strength,
forged by centuries of trials

the time is now
to shine like the brightest bonfires
and illuminate the pulsing heart

for her divinity cannot be stopped
or controlled or beat down
for the divine will always find a way

she calls her sisters
and allied brethren
as pillars of light and change

sister warriors stand tall,
stand proud, vibrate loud
within her deep abiding love

as waters of hope
the fire of change
the air of truth

remake this earth
through fertility of the the black womb
undeniable in her unstoppable force

Rise sister rise
no longer silent by greed and control
for she is the point of creation for all

She Stands

upon the hill

She stands upon the hill,
under the great and revered oak,
ancient growth in its wisdom.

Leaves falling like pearls unto her braided hair,
she weeps tears of sorrow,
a thousand stories in one salty drop.

They nurture the Earth's song
in an ever-revolving cycle
in hallowed branches.

Strong, yet fragile,
she provides shelter
from stormy skies.

The wind howls its rage,
and its benediction,
whispering edicts of creation.

She stands upon the hill,
alone, an avenging Goddess
of broken dreams.

She burns bright,
a supernova of destruction,
birthing tempered resilience forged of fire.

Forgotten, as time makes it her enemy,
she perseveres through
the endless, revolving seasons.

Never to falter,
holding strong to divinity
grounding her within stubborn roots.

She keeps knowledge and magic
of our ancestors, protecting
their light during the darkest storms.

She stands upon the hill...

Storm

there's stormy skies
brewing in my eyes
the darkest of clouds
screaming out loud

save me
save me

falling on deaf ears
losing all my years
existing in shade
while illusions fade

hear me
hear me

truth becomes lies
and there's nowhere to hide
embracing darkness
even as i confess

forgive me
forgive me

thunder crashes
lightning flashes
fracturing my soul
searing it whole

burn me
burn me

particles of electricity
attuning the frequency
surviving the storm
I am reborn

love me
love me

The Journey of a Writer
Musings

The Love Affair of Writing

Is writing an act of love?

I believe so. I think writing is a love affair, a love story, where we fall in love with our words. It's like any other relationship, full of the tumultuous ups and downs, wins and failures, rising and falling.

It started out as flirting with my words, playing around with syntaxes and rearranging verses. Perhaps it started out with a cliché or a meet-cute. It was a slow realization of the connection between me and my words, sometimes an instant spark. And, I thought, *"Hmmm...maybe there's something here."*

And there *was*.

So began the "honeymoon" phase; where I recognized this extreme passion for my words, and became completely enamored with the feeling. The rose-colored glasses shone brightly with grandiose dreams and joy. I wrote my heart out, words twitter-pated in the rush of lustful abandon. They flowed, they curved, they danced from my fingertips, spinning into works of passion. Burning bright in the explosion of creativity and ideals.

Then came the "work" phase, where I faced what was flowing and what needed to be improved upon. Where editing, rewriting, promoting, and just plain figuring-it-out came into focus. Boots to the pavement, fingers to the keyboard. Writing draft after draft, submission after submission, post after post. The process seemed relentless, and I kept encouraging myself, saying, *"But the goal is right at my fingertips!"*

At the same time, I silently wondered: *is anyone out there reading my words?*

Then I found myself at the "going-through-the motions" phase. This is where the monotony of the process tried to bury me, and dissolution surfaced. I fell into a rut. Wake, write, give a false smile, and repeat. The Inner Critic used this opportunity to restart her campaign. Eventually this phase became too uncomfortable, and staying led to a slow and torturous death–the death of creativity. It was either remain uncomfortable, or claw myself out of the dark abyss, to freedom.

And so, the "reemergence of passion" phase commenced, and I wondered why I ever felt ambivalent at all. This is where acceptance came in. This is where I embraced my authenticity, of who I was, and my role in the relationship with my words. I found that the passion was different, deeper, and more confident.

I became more experienced and stronger through embracing accountability. Admittedly, I discovered becoming accountable felt uncomfortable, but necessary. How was I to grow as a writer if I couldn't own *all* parts of my journey? The polished, the rough and the unedited. When I could wear a flashing sign that said, "This is who I am!" and *own it*.

I owned my words as a part of myself, and my journey, and a part of my truth. I came to the realization that I deserved this connection with myself.

I fought for it.

My fingers bled for it.

The last (but not least) phase of the love affair came as "gratitude." Thankful that I'd made it thus far. Finding a silver lining in all phases that I had gone through. How I laughed and cried, sang and screamed, described and ranted with my words. Finding peace in allowing appreciation for the conversation and relationship with my words that bloomed inside me and seeded out into the world.

Yet, this is a *never-ending* love affair–that of writing–where I, and my words, continue to grow and deepen in ways that are unimaginable. I look back at the love affair rollercoaster with my words and realize how far I've traveled.

I embrace how much farther I have to go.

The writing journey is not tidy, for as a writer, I am made resilient. It takes dedication, passion, gumption, and a little bit of grace. For relationships are hard, even the one with our words.

Writing is an act of love.

An endless love affair.

And as always, my journey as a writer continues.

Feed My Soul

My soul is fed
word by word
with little nuggets
of nourishment
born on creativity.

I luxuriate into
silky imagery
flowing like currents
on wind
on a lazy spring day,
only to become a maelstrom
of angst,
pushing vitriol out
stanza by stanza.

Healing is a byproduct
from digging deep into
hidden caves that house
forbidden secrets.

Pull those words out,
thrust them into light
to be cleansed
by a golden light
of truth,
making my soul burst
with renewed purpose.

Love Is a Battlefield
Poems

Absolution

You never asked for absolution.
And yet, should you?
Would I give it?
Maybe, for me,
but not for you.
I won't carry
your guilt around,
a weighted tarnished chain,
rusted and ruined.
Your punishment
is knowing that
you can never take it back.
The damage
you caused was real,
and even though we heal,
hidden scars are real.
Pink, fleshy roped lines,
scaling skin like roadmaps,
showing twisted roads
we traveled to get here.

Absolve yourself,
for even though
pain lives in both of us,
I am responsible
for absolution of mine.

Not yours, never yours.

Dreaming

I'm dreaming of you.
You know who you are,
the one who leaves a scar.
The one who pulls me in,
blaming me for your sin.

I spend dark nights dreaming,
dreams that won't leave me,
as I claw myself up, barely getting free
through your dark abyss,
hands reaching towards light's kiss.

always
dreaming

Spun softly in your world,
pieces of me fading like falling satin,
into obscurity, emotions flatten.
To grays and tans, void and dull,
as thoughts louden, my heart's resentful.

Are you dreaming of me
with your wicked tongue?
Your words were sung
over wounds down deep.
I can't get away from you even in sleep.

never
waking

Though ears are wide open,
all I see is your mesmerizing eyes,
telling me your lovely lies,
selling me your dreams,
tearing me apart at the seams.

I admit, I willingly gave in,
hoping against hope that you'd be real,
riding highs and lows of what you make me feel.
Believing you held me tightly in your grasp,
Your dreams interweave into nightmare's relapse.

currently
sleepwalking

Will I ever awaken
from this never-ending affliction?
As I make you my addiction,
I need an intervention for my soul
because without you I don't feel whole.

Dreaming through this landscape
Of soft kisses, and your colorful mosaic,
floating high in clouds, your deceptive trick.

Drowning in melting rainbows of love and pain,
I find strength to turn my back on you again.

no longer
dreaming

Emotional Bombs

A Tale of Two Fractured Souls

You fed my insecure,
damaged soul
with the dysfunction
of your love.

Craving
turned into addiction,
for that twisted validation
of my tattered self-worth.

Two magnets,
pushing,
pulling,
pushing,
pulling,
each time more explosive than the last.

Reveling in my feminine power,
I took your weakness
as my gratification,
pulling it in with greedy, needy arms.

Sitting next to you,
our legs tightly pressed together,
and yet...
I was alone
in pain and uncertainty.

Putting all my unspoken baggage
on your damaged shoulders.

That night,
when you screamed,
"Is this what you wanted?!"
my perfectly constructed
glass house shattered
in jagged, brutal self-realization.

I sat there,
alone,
surrounded by tousled sheets
in the absence
of your perfect storm.

Metaphorically
bloody and bare,
naked and stripped raw,
amidst destruction
of our emotional bombs.

Years later,
I slowly slide
into a well
of forgiveness.

A. N. TIPTON

For me,
for you,
for us,
and a war
we waged together
for our fractured souls.

Falling

I fall into pieces
when I hear your name
broken hearted
bitterness flows through my veins
I want to get past you, desperately
but I'm somehow tethered
by this addiction of you
it's not logical
I want to fall out of love with you
I might be able to outthink you any day
but my heart
is a tenacious bitch
Why won't my heart let you go?

I fall into bed
rumpled, messy, unmade
just like I've been these past weeks
because of you
eyes bleeding out pain
in wet tracks on cheeks
pulled out of the
bloody shreds of my heart
while you left me behind
day and night collide
in this revolving numbness
Why can't I forget you?

I fall into nothingness
into bleak existence
black colors my thoughts
with a heart so lonely
going through withdrawals
from your smile
smell of your skin
the feel of your heartbeat
under my ears
as you disappear from my life
leaving me adrift
alone on this river of despair
Why am I still here without you?

Forgery

Your love is a forgery,
words flowing off your tongue as honeyed silk,
they fall flat under broken promises.

The veneer of your caresses mimic authenticity
as you hand out platitudes like counterfeit bills,
empty and worthless.

After, I'm left holding an ashamed heart,
believing you to be a Rembrandt,
when you were really a pale imitation.

I see flawed lines now.
Lying in wake
of your crimes of dispassion,

I peel your lies off my skin,
revealing scars of your misleading signature,
in loops and slashes and scrupulous scrawls,
turning to phony rivulets running down into fake tattoos.

I, too, fell victim to a sham of your soft lips,
tasting like cherries, only to turn to ash under the black light,
illuminating your washed-out ink.

My salty tears mix with rain as I'm left behind alone
with my bag of hoaxes, as you disappear, the Pink Panther,
with my trust and innocence.

For you were just an illusion,
playing the strings of my heart like an out of tune violin,
taking me to undiscovered heights,

only to turn off-key,
my ears bleeding from dissonance,
breaking off pieces of a weary soul.

And now
I'm left wondering,
is all love a forgery?

Hitchhiker

I hitch. I hike.

I let the road take me places unknown.
I put my life into strangers' hands,
road sign after road sign.

Where does the road lead?
Sometimes, the road is dark and twisting,
full of pain and uncertainty.

Sometimes, I pass through purple mountains
and rolling hills of wildflowers,
with rays of sunshine following me.

Sometimes, the landscape mourns,
monotonous, listless and brown,
flat without curves.

One day, I meet him,
on the side of a dusty road,
inside a convenience store.

A package of grape gum
and Chili Cheese Fritos
fuse us together

in a conversation
that spans two states
and two nights in cheap hotels.

We were a pit stop, and we knew it,
but two days can hold a
lifetime of memories and richness.

We were meant for a fleeting experience.
Our souls said hello and goodbye again,
waiting until the next lifetime greets us.

I hitched, and then hiked,
hand waving to a pair
of worn boots behind me.

The road opens up,
yellow lines fade into the distance,
as heatwaves dance on asphalt.

For I am a hitchhiker
in this journey called life,
on a road map to places unknown.

I hitch. I hike.

My Pain

a badge of unwanted honor

You don't deserve to see my **pain**.
To you, I am nothing
but stoic, untouchable and cold
as I survive an aftermath
of a brutal war you put me through.

As tears of pain silently scream
from unseen ragged wounds,
born from tiny slices of bloody, emotional scars,
you will only see my mask of nonchalance.
For you don't deserve to see my **pain**.

Alone in darkness, I weep
scores of hot, salty rivers,
mourning who I will never be again.
For you don't deserve to see my **pain**.

I grieve the loss of innocence
and Disney dreams,
only to be born anew to another truth,

one that is part-bitter and part-cleansed.
For you don't deserve to see my **pain.**

Fires of agony have remade me
into this new mold of a person.
Someone stronger,
more resilient and compassionate.
For you don't deserve to see my **pain**.

The pain belongs to me, and me alone
as a badge of unwanted honor and bravery
amidst a landscape of my shredded heart.

Because...
You don't deserve to see my **pain**.

Since You Entered My Life

Since you entered my life,
everything has changed.
And I can't tell if it's for better or worse.

Feelings you evoke dig down deep
into my hard, encased center.

Your gentle words create long, jagged fractures,
letting wounds of the past,
feelings of the present
and hopes and fears for the future escape.

You make me *feel* again,
and part of me can't forgive you for that.

I've created a safe life for myself,
every part contained, controlled.
Predictable.

You're a messy painting,
a loud rock song,

or a summer lighting storm.
You make everything full of color, and sound, and fire.

I try desperately to close fractures,
guard my heart,
and then you come
with your sledgehammer of kisses
and soft words of love and undo it all.

It's like my heart is made of tissue paper
that you tear open so easily.
Contents spill into your lovely hands,
your sensual mouth and strong arms.

You don't want the bloody, red mess underneath.
I promise you that.
You need to walk away because I can't.
I know I should. I really should.

Then you flash your dimpled smile,
your eyes alight with unspoken things,
things I tell myself no longer exist for me,
but my feet are stuck, unable to run,
from you.

Enslaved in a promise of you,
of light shining in your soul.
It calls to me, haunting me,
slowly healing me.

Since you entered my life...

Since You Left My Life

Since you left my life, I can finally breathe.
I take in deep, clean breaths,
free of your disease.
Your chains no longer bind me in your dysfunction.
I feel lighter, freer, and somewhat fragile.

My legs are shaky, a baby fawn walking for the first time,
as I learn to walk without your suffocation.
I can now decide what I like,
not what you think I should like.
I can wear clothes I want.

I can smile at other people in stores
without being afraid of what happens when we get home.
My moods don't depend on yours, unpredictable and toxic.
I am no longer responsible for your inability to handle your life.
I can smile. I can sing. I can cook what I want.

I can have friends.
I no longer have to hide scars of your displeasure.
I can hold my head high.

I am free...
since you left my life.

Teenage Dreams

I followed my fallow heart
took a path of love and destruction
wandering upon twists and turns
through a dark forest of bare broken branches
and sunny meadow full of wildflowers

you became my all
my focal point
I gifted you my all
while believing that I only deserved
a bit of your some

I fell hard, deeply and fully
the way a teenager does
when emotions ran high and low
so full of color and sound
everything magnified to an extreme

I lost myself
in a pit of despair
with nothing to compare

in this life experience
so far

I remember you in my dreams
waiting by a phone
for the sound of your voice
a validation that I was worthy of your love
not understanding it was my love I needed

looking outwards
for something that should come from within
lessons learned through trial and error
until emotions dulled
and colors faded through a test of time

where teenage dreams
lost luster and shine
with a harshness of reality
new dreams were made
with newfound shallow maturity

Twin Flame

We might not have been together long,
but the potency of our connection
seared into memory and my heart.
It's like a bittersweet brand.

Your laugh lingers
in the hallways of my ears,
your voice remains an activation.
It's special timbre, ever-soothing.

Our souls dance in and out of many lives,
pixies in an ancient tree grove.
We are everlasting,
even in this snapshot of eternity.

Until I leave this mortal body
or until we cross another lifetime,
or timeline,
or another parallel reality,

You hold a part of me,
as I hold a part of you

Our reunion will be ever-sweet,
two ageless souls,
destined to weave throughout eternity
for our souls' evolution.

For each time, we burn fast
we burn bright,
We burn each other out
in the phoenix's fiery embrace.

We catapult each other
into growth and expansion
through love and turmoil,
too intense for any sustainable length.

Twin flames,
two halves of the same whole.

Our time has not yet come,
reflection of mine,
yin to my yang,
catalyst to my shadow...and to my light.

For, soul mine,
we are never truly alone,
throughout this immortal waltz,
because since before we were mere stardust,

sparking into life
from the great black nothingness,
and until the end of our cosmic trek,
as always,

I hold part of you
as you hold part of me.

A. N. TIPTON

Twin flames dancing
an age-old dance of existence.

Unsatisfied

she lays there
silent
taking what you give
without joy
without passion
for fear of shame
and drenched in your sullen insecurity
unsatisfied
while faking a happy ending
furthering your delusion
ignoring her self-respect
because it's expected
taking blame
of her failure
of your production
failing to live up
to unrealistic expectations
of flawed and deceptive
videos on a screen
is she a whore or prude?

there is no in-between
no where for her to go
up or down
wrong or wrong
and so she shuts down
"you're so cold"
"like a fish"
"not my fantasy"
"can't you just lay there?"
she ignores the empty space
in her heart
in her womb
for your satisfaction
finally, curling up to her side
along your sweaty skin
feeling diminished
and carefully
- nothing-
in her waking dream

The Journey of a Writer
Musings

When You've Hit A Dry Spell

Have you ever experienced those times when words refuse to come out and play? The blank page, a blinking cursor taunts, as your brain or heart tries to emerge some freaking emotion or thought onto the page. But to no avail.

Nothing.
Nada.
Zilch.

Blankness becomes your friend. It's extremely frustrating.

This is what I've been going through. The funny thing is that my brain constantly creates stories and ideas, but when I sit down to write...*poof*. Gone.

I wonder, *am I broken?*

I see writer friends publish books, or post piece after piece on Medium or other online platforms, and I ask myself, *how do they have the time?* Between a day job, taking care of my family, getting my kid ready for a new school year, and fighting competing crowded spaces in my brain, I'm spent.

My Inner Critic whispers sly doubts into my ear, but we've played this game before. I'm not feeding into it. Nope, not this time. My Muse jumps on my shoulder, hands on hips, ready to defend. I feel I might go after my Inner Critic, broom swinging in violent abandon.

But, I contain myself.
Barely.

I realized that I've hit a dry spell...with my words. Creativity has been a Mojave Desert. Little bursts of inspiration come, get creative juices flowing, and then an excuse, obstacle, or insecurity pops up and...**BAM**. Full stop. I mean, come on! Enough is enough already.

This is the time where I stop, and allow myself a little grace. I stop comparing myself to others and remind myself that my writing journey is my own. I surrender and work on releasing any and all judgment. *I freaking relax.*

I find that current times are chaotic. The world is pulled in so many directions, as is humanity. I'm overwhelmed by the War of Words flashing across screens everywhere. There's divisiveness and fear.

It's time to go within and ground. It's time to remember that I am a creative being. I stop trying to force words, sit back, and allow them to come.

It's hard. The more vulnerable I feel, the more repressed and agitated I become, the more I want to control things. These lead to stress, and stress is no place for creation.

I consciously have to remind myself to relax and trust my connection to words.

So, if I give myself a little time out, that's okay.

The words will find me when I'm ready. And the dry spell? I'll know when the time is right to end it.

And as always, my journey as a writer continues.

A Letter To My Muse

a benediction of sorts

Dear Muse,

It's been a while since I've reached out to you, or since I've been willing to listen. I wish I could say I have an excuse. I'm sure I can conjure up some lame ones for you, but the reality is that I lost my way. Maybe I've been in a time of reflection instead of expression. I'll admit, I allowed exhaustion to get me. Completely. Utterly. Dejectedly.

My first instinct is to offer platitudes, to say that I know you have my back and want what's best for me. But the honest, gritty truth is I became overwhelmed. The constant inundation from social media, and trying to balance my creativity with the demands of full time work and family, took their toll.

Please don't be disappointed because I'm struggling not to feel disappointed in myself. I told myself that I needed some "me" time. That something had to give. That the outside world, the constant barrage of mainstream media, social media, fear mongering, and a world on fire, didn't affect me. That me, as a chill and positive person, didn't fall prey to the collective consciousness, fueled by anxiety.

But I'd be lying. Days turned into weeks and then into months, and I couldn't bring myself to listen to you. I turned off my ears and shuffled through a haze of monotony (and probably a bit of depression) from morning to night, in an oblivion of survival.

The Inner Critic grew big and plump from all that it fed me, and I consumed more than I should have. My stories' characters whispered to me, and begged me to give them life. Later, I whispered, like the sweetest of lies, and fell back into escape.

I became a hermit, existing alone amongst those who orbited me. I smiled a brittle smile, and disappeared down into an abyss, cocooned in a darkness. It paraded as safety, when it was really a prison.

Until enough was enough.

I know I'm lucky, Muse. Life could've been worse, right? Others have it worse. And yet, I wonder, what does it take to succeed? How do I measure my level of writing success? Is it how many articles, stories, books or poems I publish? Is it the amount of pennies I make? Is it how many 'friends' or 'followers' I have? Or is it how happy I am? Is success measured by how much my heart sings in celebration of my creations?

When do ambition and drive, goals and dreams, get pushed aside for survival's sake? When do the sick and twisted standards that I impossibly impose become debilitating? Who am I to have the audacity to feel this way?

Muse, for months I was on a creative high. You cheered me on. And then...silence. Did I reach a level of comfort and fall flat? Did I give up and settle? Did I let the Inner Critic get too far into my head? How do I tear down walls of self-judgment I spent years erecting? Muse, am I alone in feeling this way?

These questions are burned into my brain, begging old, outdated, neural pathways to give way to new ones. Perhaps the temptation to fall back into a familiar rut was too enticing.

But, Muse, this is me...reaching out to you. I want to be ready to listen. I believe in you, I do. I know you believe in me, too. Do you forgive me for ignoring you?

I'm trying to forgive myself. Maybe there's nothing to forgive. And yet, thoughts of inadequacy and failure haunt me.

Today I'm writing this letter to you. I'm showing up, when I want to disappear. So, please, don't give up on me. I'm breaking the chains, link by link if needed, to let words out.

I'm bearing my soul, not so much as a cry for help, but as a benediction. Please, be patient. Like many others, I'm a work-in-progress. I'm digging deep to find passion, that small ember that burned down low and got covered by cold ash. And yet, it never went out. Help me fan the flame, Muse. Help me find my words again.

I'm here, I'm ready, and I'm listening.

With all the words and love in my heart,
Me

Welcome to Shadowland

Poems

A Blessing Retracted

She cries
from an empty womb,
carried away
from the
crimson flow,
of no more,
of never to be,
of dreams dashed
and expectations crashed
into contractions
of grief.

I hear her cries,
or are they mine?
Unable to deny
the truth
of my heart
emptying,
my soul now fractured
from her

unexpected,
expected departure.

She has no name,
a destiny unfulfilled
as
what might have been
or
who she might have become,
only to cease
existing.

Where words
like
not viable
and
mis-carry
carry her away
from my forever
empty arms.

Was she to be
an Isabella,
or an Indigo,
or an Alina,
depleted from
a mother's hope,
blind sided by
cruelty
of a moment of
truth?

Emptiness
has taken on new meaning
where emotions
are riotous,
feeling loss
of her spirit
flowing down
black,
swirling abyss
as the body deflates
of
no beating heart.

Days are dark,
existing
in tunnel vision
as the world spins
on the outside
- round and round -
in a haze
of numb hands
and placating,
well-meaning words

until...
an acquaintance springs
upon my tattered soul
a spontaneous prayer,
not of my faith,
but fueled by
the purity of their faith,
offering a brief moment
of abiding peace.

115

How can one
say goodbye
when there was
no hello?
Dearly departed
into
never was,
never will be,
but never forgotten
imprinting
a deep ichor
bruise
upon this fallow heart

An angel,
a gift ungiven,
a blessing retracted,
as her spirit
gets spirited away
unto mercy's
warm embrace,
leaving behind
coldness
of the long,
desolate,
barren winter.

And despite,
or perhaps
in spite,
I survive
through
bleak emptiness

to live another day,
day after day,
wading through fields
of grief
as any mother
would.

Never to know
her mind,
her smell,
her laughter,
her tears,
her stamp on this
unforgiving world,
but only the
ghost of
what could have been
and will never be.

My daughter.

Empty

Empty, like my eyes
dead of night
falling down in a dark abyss

Grief is that
feeling of nothingness
after a storm of pain of loss

Limbs moving without purpose
motions autopilot
yet life keeps moving

Even though I'm empty
a lifeless existence
after the spark of life fades

I've felt it all
hope, excitement, joy,
then shock, hopelessness...pain

Coming in waves
of forcibly letting go
of dreams, of love

Tears still flow
even though the morning's gray
fading into obscurity

Hollowed out
insides scooped raw
until they are tender things

I welcome emptiness
a nothingness with
the passing of time

Colors are muted
disconnected from time
alone in a sea of others

My heart feels
like my arms
Empty

Endless Dreams

here I go
disappearing again
into a riptide
of anonymity.

I vacillate between
here and there,
never really anywhere
but inside my head.

I pull the covers
over my head
feel the dread
seeping in like
spectral fingers.

where darkness
is a solace
comforted by numbness
invading my soul.

here we go
down a rabbit hole
where no wonderland
truly exists within this
weary heart.

and existence becomes
a litany of flipping calendar pages
passing aimlessly by
with all my regrets.

waiting for rays
of the sun
to chase the night away
of this endless dream.

Home

a place
from where I exist
in these maze of walls
and rooms separated by purpose.

purposeless,
watching the tube
hypnotized by endless
pharmaceutical commercials

tell me,
what is wrong with me,
what ailments can I manifest
to feed your greed

a buzz
of little black boxes
spreading emf frequencies
eating up oxygen

I hear you
ringing in my ears

diluting my cells
dumbing me down, down, down

until I wake up
to slave away in my cubicle
trapped in the same revolving day
of mediocrity

to go home
with the same four walls,
my prison of time
wasted on your propaganda

happy and plump
with your addiction,
swiping up, down, left, right
into a vortex of unremembering

as my soul screams
its silent scream
WAKE UP
while I scroll along within the dream

Nothing

I feel nothing,
flat,
a plateau,
barren, cracked earth,
parched,
color leaks out,
rivulets of blood like passion
falling through cracks.

Inundated with chaos
all around me,
pressure squeezing like a vice,
pushing me towards
complacency.
it would be easier
to comply,
to give in,
follow in footsteps
of those asleep.

I want to sleep,
in the convenience of
hope of safety.
Giving up freedoms,
small bite sizes,
like lobsters
in a slow, warm bath,
comforted,
until we realize
we are boiling.

Too late,
too much sacrifice,
until we are empty husks,
a commodity to be
bought and sold.
like our health.

I feel nothing,
dragged down into an abyss,
where darkness embraces us,
death's loving wings,
bleeding us dry.
My soul cries out,
black maw of a mouth
disjointed, wide open,
screaming silently,
WAKE UP.

I feel nothing,
until it's all I know,
pain and suffering is
now currency,

becoming little assets
belonging...
not to ourselves.
Enslavement
never looked so good
with those who
vow to keep us safe,
where,
I feel nothing.

Merrily Life Is But A Dream

but is it?

Am I sleepwalking
through this dream called life?
What is real or imagined?
Most of what we experience is a dream,
the mass hypnosis of viral programming.

What if clocks were designed
to keep us ticking and tocking along,
never to question those twinges we feel?
When the world shifts and bends
outside our norm,
do our eyes see the reality of it?
Unused to the oddities
and divergence from normality,
we shuffle forward on numb feet.

I think I fell asleep
around seven years-old,
integrated into "normal" society,
realizing that the world

didn't see truth as I did.
And so,
I succumbed to the dream,
this thing we call living,
but what if we are really sleeping?
And if so, how do I wake?

Eyes wide open,
yet closed to what could be seen.
Ears hearing, but unable to listen
amidst a hum
of electromagnetic influences.
Existing between multiple realities
fluctuating between frequencies
in our waking dreams.

Merrily,
or perhaps not,
life is but a dream.

Secrets

a dark poem

She wants to unearth her secrets
rotting, little coffins
in a cemetery of truths
where traumas stay hidden
in crevices of her mental maze.

Wrong turns and dead ends
shield a path to center
where nightmares
and healing
can be found.

She sees shifting walls
built in steel,
and fear,
and cotton candy,
keeping herself safe.

She has learned that trust
is a sick game,
and love

is a commodity,
and her light and essence
are eaten away
by greedy, diseased things.

She finds that
her strength
was forged
by fire
and psychological games.

Her secrets are wrapped up
like bubble wrap
insulated by worlds created
from within
her inner sanctuary
until she creates her own truths.

So...
she reimagines other secrets
that tell a story
she wishes into being,
so they become
her secrets
unearthed.

That Time I Was a Child

That time I was a child,
what seems
another lifetime now
and I wonder,
was I ever really a child
to see the things I saw?
You see me
sweet,
or innocent,
something to be protected
because I molded my image
to your expectations,
a personality,
cocooned in an
illusionary protection
that I created.

That time I was a child,
I learned
to not trust,
that everyone lies,

that I'm on my own
in a den of wolves,
creating safety
in fantasies and escapism.
I see no evil.
I hear no evil.
I speak no evil
...silenced.

That time I was a child,
I was told
to be quiet.
I was told
I was selfish.
I was told,
never depend on a man
to take care of you.
Dreams deflated,
with a fantasy
I so desperately
wanted to hold onto
was ripped to shreds,
doused with an
ice-cold bucket
of reality.

That time I was a child,
I wasn't
really a child at all.
I was purity,
squeezed tight,
tamped down,
repressed,

molded,
compliable,
by bitterness
and perhaps fear.

That time I was a child
has come and gone,
like ashes
floating on wind,
disappeared as if it never existed,
until that child
is buried
deep, *deep,* deep
down.
Hidden away
in a sacred chamber
of the heart,
waiting
in shifting shadows,
yearning to be liberated.

That time I was a child.

The Lunar Call

I call out to the elusive Moon,
Don't you love me?
Don't you want me?
There's barely any light tonight,
the Moon is unapproachable.
A little piece of my heart cries out
as I fold into myself.

Tonight,
is a rare blue Moon.
A silvery glow lights the night sky,
like a small flame of hope in my chest.
Does love taste like mint chocolate chip ice cream?
The Moon shines bright in that single magical moment,
that I wonder if the Moon loves me?

The next time I waited for fullness,
I found a sliver,
It's back, turned and cold,
allowing the darkness to infiltrate.
And I know...

the Moon doesn't love me.
Why am I not good enough for its beauty?

The Moon gives its light grudgingly,
it wonders why I shy away.
Now I wonder,
am I not a good companion to the Moon?
Maybe I should just be happy with
what little light the Moon gives me?
My worth is tied to the wax and wane.

Phases come and go,
rotating around the many cycles of my life
and I realized the wars
the Moon has faced.
That the Moon kept its light contained,
for the Moon had demons too.
The Moon didn't love itself.

Regardless of the Moon's reasons,
its actions left me desolate and sad.
It abandoned me,
over and over,
in its lunar rotation.
Emotionally unavailable and
I suffered.
Greatly.

I questioned my worth.
I believed that
if I was a good companion,
then the Moon would love me.
If I was perfect,

the Moon would pay attention to me.
I would matter.

And at the same time,
I want to yell,
"Screw you, Moon!"
Why doesn't the Moon
show me how little I mean,
compared to its
feelings and demons?

How it's always my job
to call out to the Moon,
and then it makes me feel bad
when I stop calling out.
What does it expect?
No really, I want to know,
what does the Moon expect?

And now I turn my back
to the haunting lunar call,
now shining
with full and robust beams,
wondering if lunar cycles
have made me a bit
of a lunatic.

The Rearview Mirror

Oh, little girl,
crystal tears on her cheeks,
his face, almost a memory
in the rearview mirror.
Not once does he look back,
spelling a bitter goodbye,
as he drives away.
Bright tail lights flash in broken finality,
hopeless, red and white,
blinking away rain
like her tears,
as if she meant nothing.
Was it easy for him to just walk away, to give her up?

Oh, little girl,
trying hard to prove her worth,
to win,
to earn,
to yearn for his approval.
Desperately begging for any small scrap,

only to realize it was an impossible feat.
She wasn't loved enough,
or good enough,
to be loved.
So, she learned never to hope,
that expectations are a disappointing luxury.
She keeps her head down,
falls into the cracks,
disappears like dust motes
through an elusive ray of sun
peeking through drabby mustard-colored curtains.
His face, now a memory,
in the rearview mirror.

The Journey of a Writer
Musings

The Voice of the Writer

Have you thought about your voice as a writer? How words flow and come together as a unique extension of yourself? I imagine that for some people, finding their voice comes easy, while for others, it takes exploration. I admit that for me, finding my voice takes exploration. I say this in the present tense, because I feel that I'm constantly evolving and growing as a writer.

Another milestone of my writing journey was learning the difference between *who I wanted to be* and *who I was* as a writer in terms of voice. Maybe each wordsmith comes to his or her own realization at some point in their writing, perhaps sometimes repeatedly.

Years ago in my writing journey, I joined a critique group of fiction writers. We all wrote in the same genre. Each time we met we had to submit a chapter, and then provide feedback to one another. The exchanges had been one of the most amazing experiences I'd had in my writing experience up to that point. Prior to then I'd remained a lonely, closet writer. The first time I shared my work, which felt like revealing a piece of me, was nerve-racking. But I found that there was something to be said about collaborating and co-creating in a group, especially if each person was adding their unique perspective. When a piece of writing dwells in our heads too long, what we think comes across, and what people actually perceive, can be completely different. Others' perspectives, if provided through honest, positive feedback, can be invaluable.

There is a magic that happens when receiving and acknowledging another's work, while simultaneously being seen and heard through your own. When I joined that group, I wanted to write like my favorite authors. I wanted to be a badass, and create worlds, characters, and stories like them. I wanted to create fight scenes, and create sarcastic, witty characters. I found out the hard way, writing from emulation didn't work like that.

At least not for me.

What I discovered was that the words and voices that emerged from me were completely different from my thoughts. My style of writing worked better when I didn't force the words into what I *thought* they should be. Truthfully, I can see now that I didn't want to accept my own voice. The Inner Critic had many things to say about how *my* voice wouldn't be accepted, and about how it would be judged and ostracized. My Inner Critic whispered that I was fooling myself, that I didn't have it in me to follow through, and that staying safe was the right thing to do.

In hindsight, I had to learn how to be true to myself, and how to accept all the parts of myself. I had to *find* and *discover* who I was through my words: the good parts and not-so good parts. I had to allow my words a voice, their most *authentic* voice. I had to dig deep to find the courage and power from inside in order to shove my Inner Critic off the metaphorical cliff *(again)*.

I had to *own* my words, claim them, and claim the beauty that was, and is, *me*.

Sounds easy, right? Ha! I think anytime one steps out of their comfort zone growth follows. And, growth can be good, but sometimes it's painful and un-comfortable. Sometimes we have to let go of the old to make room for the new, and for what's buried deep down inside. This includes the secrets that we keep from ourselves, and use words to have that conversation with yourself.

This is what I'm discovering.

My voice is my own. My writing was, is, and will always be an extension of me. Sure, I could learn the craft and hone skills here and there, but allowing my voice freedom to fly, to be heard, that's the real lesson. This awareness took time. It's exploring different types and styles of writing, and pushing beyond a dreaded comfort zone. Sometimes I'm not happy with what comes from trying something new. Sometimes I'm shocked by the texture of words that come through. Sometimes I share my words and people like them. Go figure.

So, yeah, I think about my voice as a writer. I practice allowing words to flow *through* me, instead of pushing them out, and I make room for those times when I do give a push, a nudge, or an occasional shove to get creative juices flowing.

I'm still learning, exploring, playing, and creating on this journey as a writer.

And as always, my journey as a writer continues.

A Letter To My Inner Critic

a realization of sorts

Dear Inner Critic,

I know who you are. I see you.

I hear you, your voice flows like a mantra in my head. You whisper lies to me as a form of protection. You fuel self-doubt and fear like wildfires. You reinforce conformity of my choices, and where logic overrides passion.

And I've listened to you, my Inner Critic.

I've believed your honeyed words that seduced me to dim my inner light, and encouraged me to slow the flow of my words in creative abandon.

I understand that you were created to keep me safe, but also to instill limiting beliefs I have ascribed to. I see that you are the voice born from insecurities and doubts, fears and disappointments.

Your purpose is to show me the shadow of myself.

Perhaps you unknowingly provided a gift to better know myself. For how can I be a conduit of my words if I didn't fully embrace the fullness of your purpose? To accept *that I am human, living a human experience. That there is purpose in dark, as well as in light. You've shown me the dark, Inner Critic.*

Perhaps the lies you whisper are the opposite truths of my soul. When you hint that my writing isn't good enough, or that no one will read it, I let those beliefs hold me back. When you remind me that I can't make a career from writing, I give in to the fears of financial insecurity. When you recommended putting away the manuscript that I toiled over for seven years, I listened. I lean into the imposter syndrome time and time again.

And that's okay, Inner Critic. I choose not to be angry, but instead I choose gratitude. You have a job, and at times you've served me well. I'm learning not to run from you, or shut you off, but to fully embrace you with love and compassion from my heart. Perhaps together we'll find our voices, our words, so we can continue to co-create.

Were you ever jealous of the Muse? Don't be. She is part of me, just like you are. Where she encourages me to flourish, you give opportunities to grow. You both serve me in different ways. I now know not to take your words at face value, but to peek behind the shadows of what needs to be purged, loved, and forgiven.

Our relationship is a work in progress, Inner Critic. I no longer want to hold onto the limiting beliefs that hold me back. A first step is recognizing them, acknowledging them, and then releasing them, over and over again, until they fade into obscurity. You're helping me with that.

I want to thank you, my beautiful Inner Critic, for giving me the opportunity to overcome any obstacles so my voice can be heard. You unknowingly deepened my relationship with my words, and allowed me to explore different facets of myself for this journey. Now when you speak, I listen, but I listen differently. I examine the meaning or feeling behind your whispers.

I don't always get it right. Sometimes I let your whispers take hold before I realize it. And that's okay, because my Muse is also here to remind me that I am a mosaic of different colors. And so, I feed those hues into my words, to weave a beautiful, haunting tapestry of poems, musings, fiction, and more.

While I don't always love your purpose, your taunts, your whispers, I accept that you are a part of me who needs love, acceptance, and forgiveness. I accept that you have a role to play in this amazing journey that I'm on, this journey of a writer.

So, for now, I may hear you, but will I listen in the same way?

We shall see.

With all the words and love in my heart,

Me

Emerging Through the Shadows
Poems

I Am

I am strong.
Strong as an ancient oak tree
willing to bend, but not break.
I can withstand anything,
the storms, wind and rain...
for I am strong.

I am determined.
Determined as the wind.
I will howl and rage for what I want,
but I am also gentle and soft.
I may not always be noticed,
but I am always there...
for I am determined.

I am honest.
Honest as a mirror.
Never shunning truth
but looking squarely into it.
I show reality, created from a truth within

and release visions based off fear...
for I am honest.

I am passionate.
Passionate as the sea.
Always feeling with warmth,
but also with cold.
I take many things,
but I am always giving in return...
for I am passionate.

I am human.
Human as everybody else.
I have a body and a mind,
but also a spirit.
I am perfect in my imperfections and
the best that I can possibly be.
I strive for meaning and answers...
for I am human.

I am.

Change Is Gonna Come

I want, no I need, to move forward
to shed the old
so, my feet move to take a step
my knees locking in denial

I stretch for the horizon, hands splayed
towards a new path
but cobwebs of the past
cling to me like sticky fingers

I realize, in order to change
I need to disentangle silky threads, one by one
they are tenacious, clinging to me
tiny razor, sharp claws
but I choose one and acknowledge it

I learn to forgive
accept that it has played a part in my story
one I once transcribed to believe
a hardcore truth
and yet, now I have a choice

A. N. TIPTON

I can choose a different story
a new story
my story
full of hope, and new beginnings

that thread grudgingly releases
with bitter defeat
it was hard, facing that truth
which my eyes were blind to

again, I push forward
groping for change
the cobwebs snatch me back
so, I dig deep, down the spiral

struggling to find another truth
another old belief, or pattern
that I can part with
there

that one is red and gnarly
pain pulses down its length
like a dark heartbeat

I take a deep, slow breath
full of light and determination
and rip it off, a band aid

another violent release
and I feel, with each thread
a bit more
feather light.

Light Abides

Where light abides
and darkness hides,
hidden within the same chambers,
as I compartmentalize.

As yin and yang
no one to blame
as these things that exist
in a dance without a name.

Day by day I vacillate
back from love to hate
as my divinity breaks through
and my shadows abate.

Not black or white
or wrong or right
but forged as one
through this tumultuous fight.

I stand up tall
as I crumple and fall

accumulating wisdom and strength
because of it all.

Where light abides
and darkness hides
upon this weary soul
unfractured by two sides.

I Fall

I fall,
into endless stars of your eyes,
fathomless pits of desire.

~

I fall,
away from the easy things,
choosing to shred my emotions instead.

~

I fall,
through a looking glass,
my reflection is just an illusion
for the world to see.

~

I fall,
as if there was no tomorrow,
over a cliff into the deep blue sea.

~

I fall,
from grace, moving though and accepting
the shame of choices based on ego.

~

I fall,
into insanity,
making the same damn choices,
on repeat.

~

I fall,
over my feet, to get to you,
or maybe away from myself.

~

I fall...

It's Time To Wake Up Now

Down a rabbit hole I go,
a spiral staircase,
broken and solitary.
Forced to confront
hidden truths
in the depths of my soul.
Unworthy. Unloved. Undesired.
Believing lies
that I tell myself,
that others tell me,
not in their words
but in their actions.
Undeniable.

Light streams through
the tattered holes
in this dark psyche I exist in.
Truth reaches for me,
shines on me,
tells me I'm not alone.

I turn away,
comfortable in fear,
my denial,
falsehoods clinging to me.
It's easier to believe lies,
then confront truth.
Wrapping them around me
like a cold blanket ,
shivering in darkness.
My familiar companion.

Teardrops freeze
on alabaster cheeks,
hardened by years
of viral programming.
Who will save me?
No one can save me.
I am the only one
who can save me.
But I am weak.
Or so I tell myself.

Who is this broken soul,
who hides within traumas of old?
Shards of mirrored perceptions,
twisted to accommodate
fear and chaos and
flimsy illusion of ego,
litter the barren ground.

"You are loved, beloved,"
the voice sings to me
in the dark recesses,

bathing me with light and truth.
It hurts, the truth,
voices of angels.
It's too much, too good,
I want to believe.
Only I can choose to.

I pull coldness closer,
reaching for nonexistent
warmth promised to me.
Empty, hollow promises.
Truth arises,
like a lone, green shoot
forcing its way
up through
barren land.

Only I can break
self-imposed shackles.
The ties that bind.
The self-imposed slavery.

"You are Divine,
Sovereign,
Powerful,
Remember," they sing.
Ancient songs,
long forgotten,
trapped in a corrupted
core of our very existence.
The truth
written by stars,

of our own universe,
waiting to be set free.

> "It's time to wake up, now,
> Sweet child," the song persists,
> vibrating within my soul.
> I drop the cold blanket,
> woven from dark falsehoods.
> It's only one baby step,
> but for now,
> it's enough.

For I am enough.

We are all enough.

Let Me Begin Again

Let me begin again
rising up and out
of forced imprisonment
of ideals and wants
let me erase words of yesterday
misspoken in heated incongruence

Let me begin again
to rediscover and unearth
those parts of myself
that I buried with misconception
that you being uncomfortable
was more important
than truth

Let me begin again
by mourning all I had lost
by choice or circumstance
and guilt that lives
within those experiences
I begin,

and begin
and regress out of fear
and then begin in a cycle of
insanity and sheer stubbornness
pulled up by bootstraps
putting on my big girl pants
I am beginning again

Let me begin again
this time let me embody
all parts of me
the powerful
fractured and broken
oppressor and oppressed
victim of my own making
and triumphant heart
that still bleeds to this day

Let me begin again
stand aside me
or behind me
or in front of me
as a statue of times past
a reflection of missteps
but no longer in relation
to an inside of me
I care not
as long as I begin again

Metamorphosis

The truth, unfettered.
They said I was small,
unworthy and selfish,
I took those words as if they belonged.
Who was I to shine my light?

To be... and smile... and dream.

Somehow those inconsequential words
gained power,
burrowing into crevices of self-worth.
Years went by, passing like rain.
Until you.

"You're beautiful," you said.
I barely dared to believe.
How would you know?

"You are worthy," you said.
And an unexpected truth
breathed new life into my soul.

I consecrated into me
the new truth, bit by bit,
mile by painful mile.

A new truth of self-worth
wove into the genome of my soul,
into the fabric of my DNA.

Unfettered self-love birthed
a new being of metamorphosis
embodied by divinity within.

I was made anew,
stretching out new membranes
and multicolored scales
transformed into higher consciousness.

Bursting free,
floating on translucent wings,
forged of strength and perseverance,
upon light waves of love and undiluted truths.

Now *I say*,
I am powerful, worthy, and abundant.
I lay claim to these words, for
I am **here** to shine my light.
To be... and smile... and dream.

Repent

I repent,
not for my sins,
but sins of others
who thought
they could
oppress
the divinity of
humanity.

I repent,
unto myself
of thoughtless
deeds,
and words,
infectious and
invasive like a virus,
that I beheld upon others.

I repent,
for damage
I've inflicted upon myself

under falsity of
force-fed beliefs
for which my heart
rebelled in its
intuitive wisdom.

I repent,
for selfishness
of standing up for
my needs
in a home
of broken souls,
begging for light
and love
and redemption.

Finally,
why should I repent?
Instead,
I choose
to boldly stand
for *all* colors,
light or dark,
revolving hues
that shine in varying
vibrations,
encompassing
all that
I am.

Something Began When

Something began
when meteors fell from the sky.
Some say it was magic,
some say it was a blessing,
some say it was a curse,
some say it was the end of times.
But I knew in my heart of hearts
that nothing would be the same again.
I felt it down to my very bones,
like a resonance from a gong,
or singing bowl,
like a premonition.
Something was coming,
or came,
that would change the fabric of reality.
As time went by,
we prayed to go back to how it was before.
We could hold fast
to a past
that was already lost,

with greedy, grasping hands,
we held it close to our chests,
like flimsy armor,
as if it could save us somehow
if only we believed hard enough.
But it was too late.
The change snuck upon us,
hidden in plain sight,
insidious to some,
but salvation for others.
Now we sit around a fire,
huddled for comfort and warmth,
and talk about the night meteors fell from the sky,
as if we could contain it.
Put it back into a box.
Shut our eyes to reality a little while longer.
Dreaming a dream
that no longer existed.
Hoping against all hope
that the change
wouldn't become a nightmare,
but our saving grace.

That Once Child

I saw you as a child
buried deep within a scarred man
innocent,
needing love and attention

I forgot
who you once were
amongst ravages of time
was it was a remembrance
or a benediction
or memories deeply hidden

who says what we become
from life
from choices
thrust upon us by others
and then our own

are you finding that once child
or was it a reminder
what was a glimpse

the curtain parted
to let innocence shine through

whatever the reason
it was a given gift
a reminder reminding
a chance at forgiveness
for you, for me, for expansion

to know that
whatever we have become
the core of us is pure
I see you
as you were

the divine truth of who you are
stripped-down essence
of childlike innocence
exuding freedom of love
wanting to be loved

the heart opens
slightly wider
softens with compassion
remembering
remembering
remembering

as gratitude flows
through me
deep within
a dream I dreamt of you
of that once child

The Journey of a Writer
Musings

My Relationship with Writing

Why do I write?

What is my relationship to writing?

When I was younger, writing was a way to express myself. To get out pent-up emotions and frustrations boiling inside. But writing was also something very private. It was only for me — the deep, deep, deep-down me that no one was allowed to see. Being seen by the world wasn't always safe. It wasn't safe to show myself. Or so I thought.

Writing was always associated with reading. Stories were my salvation, my escape, my hope, my teachers, my mentors. I fell in love. With characters. With worlds. With relationships, all penned on paper.

Then I reached deeper still, and recognized that I wanted to be a writer. Or, maybe even an author. That was if I'd been brave enough to let words out of the private prison, or sanctuary, that I'd kept them in.

I found that other authors, poets and writers —were my people. My tribe. Maybe hiding my words was the same as hiding myself. I was a shy, introverted kid. However, there was a part of me that didn't want to hide. I'd wanted, no *needed*, to be heard, and speak *my* truth. Not for anyone else but me.

The question was presented...*what do I want from my relationship with writing?*

An answer emerged...

I want to change my relationship with my writing. I want to soar. I want to yell from high on a mountain, and have my words pour out of me. I resolve to beat the Inner Critic, like a ninja, like a kung-fu master, bludgeon it to pieces. Break it down and then rebuild the relationship into my own creation. I want to be brave. I don't want to talk about writing, but actually write.

I am doing it.
I want to believe it.
I do believe.
I have no choice but to believe.

Or, I could sink into mediocrity, and talk about inaction to death, and about the inaction of living up to my writing potential. I could talk about self-sabotage from fear, a fear that ruled me, caged me, and tore me down. I see, my relationship to writing is my relationship to myself.

There is no separation.

The words are my ego, my fears, and my humanness from this experience of life.

The words are my soul, my higher perspective, the divine being trapped inside a living temple.

All of them belong to, and express through, the same me.

When I am truly authentically writing, it comes from a place of trust that was carefully cultivated from my relationship with words. Part of that trust was, and is, learning to surrender to an unfettered flow from within. Practicing becoming an open vessel or conduit for my inner voice. And, being willing to listen.

Words that arise deepen my understanding of myself; allow forgotten or hidden parts of myself to emerge. Sometimes new parts of me are discovered and expand through the act of creation.

I want my relationship with writing to be
expansive,
creative,
beautiful,
haunting,
chaotic,
resonant,
emotive,
and free.

I want to keep feeling the creative energy spiral up into something new or reimagined. I want the highs and lows of weaving words upon a page to take me on a wild journey.

Like all relationships, a relationship with writing is an ever-changing, ever-evolving process, worthy of my time, my attention, and my **love**.

And as always, my journey as a writer continues.

What Writing Means To Me

it means
freedom
Expression
being able to breathe
at long last
not holding it in
Escape
into another world
to touch a life
of another person
to feel what they feel
to touch my own feelings
Emote
to heal
to journey
to twist, wind, turn
and fly
Explore
other worlds
real or fantasy

the roller coaster
of relationships
mine, yours, others
a kaleidoscope
of landscapes
shifting seasons
all the colors
Exhale
out pain
grief
joys
as words
on paper
on a screen
scratching
tap-tap-tapping
Exhume
dig it out
from the root
to the light of day
release it
into the world
Expose
Embrace

Into The Divine
Poems

My Morning Prayer

My morning prayer
starts in this field
of emerald pastures
rolling under a rising sun.

The earth greets me,
a long lost lover,
welcomes me into
her warm embrace.

I give thanks
for this sacred moment
of reflection.
I let words spill
onto a page,
not knowing
what will come.

The earth asks me
to name my fears.

My soul whispers softly,
of being seen
of what people may think
of being bound by
old thought patterns
or past transgressions
or unrealized fears

I ask to be unbound.
I ask for courage
and knowing
and confidence
to step out and
SPEAK, WRITE, CREATE
and know that it is safe.

I give these fears,
excuses,
limitations
to the earth now
and she takes them
down into a pulse of
her heart center,
transmutating,
eradicating,
eliminating their hold.

I open wide
gently
to new possibilities
Gaia's voice, whisper soft
breathes her eternal love
through me.

I drop into my grateful heart
within this connection
of oneness
with the knowing
that I was heard.

So I close
in benediction,
So be it
And so it is

My Religion Is

My religion is
the embodiment of love,
an elusive divinity that
hides within
our sentient hearts,
like a starving flame
begging
to burn bright.

My religion is
the smile
in my baby's eyes,
windows of innocence
an unfettered soul,
pure,
before an infection
of humanity
can take hold.

My religion is
the forest who

listens to my grief
and sorrow,
silent companions,
laying compassion
on my weary soul
like an invisible embrace.

My religion is
a blanket of stars
that bear witness
upon my life
as I weave and meander
through repercussions from
choices I've made.

My religion is
the solace of
faces around me
who offer
small acts of kindness
as silent benedictions
in this unhinged world.

My religion is
my own,
worshiping upon
an altar of
All That Is.
That which comforts
and carries me
upon wings of
holy fire,

breathing hope
into my burdened heart.

Remember

I breathe,
sacred breath,
hallowed be thy silence
weighted by the infinite.
Divinity awakened,
through the very fabric
of my existence.
threads,
multihued by a
rainbow spectrum.

I honor
that which is,
and breathes
life
through words.
Out through my fingers
into the world,
an invasion
of light,
a light bringer,

to our addiction
to darkness.

We've forgotten,
by generational accord.
But no more,
for we are here
to remember.
I breathe new life
into perspective
infusing light bodies
and dense bodies
a time of remembrance.
a way of new.
Behold,
I make all things new.

You
have power
you have always
been powerful.
Divine.
Worthy.
Activate
that which is your
divine inheritance
so we may
choose light
instead of replaying
stories of distant
pasts.

We are one,
in all our glory,
and abundance,
and beingness.
You
are your savior.
Remember.

Starseed

I stand on this world
but I am not of this world
I am an imposter on this planet
playing out an incarnation
the self of me that has forgotten
misses the stars
it misses space and emptiness
I look up at twinkling dots in the sky
long dead, burnt out stars
barren craters of the moon
and I long for home

But I am here
a light in the dark expanse of humanity
my soul chose this
even when it's foreign
even when I know it's for expansion
for expansion's sake
when I know it's a dark night of existence
to survive it, experience it
a matrix of darkness, of starkness,

of long forgotten magic
that has been oppressed
and mutated, and pushed down
in this evolution called humanity

The stars sing out their songs
calling me home
to a home I no longer inhabit
existing only in
fading dreams upon waking
constellations hidden by
cloudy skies and light pollution
I yearn for wide, mountain skies
with swirls of midnight
indigo
violet rays as pinpricks
beaming through the velvety night
bringing me closer to
my soul's reunion
within the expanse
of stars

The Art of Surrendering

I'm constricting
my insides squeeze
press me down
I'm spiraling
greedily clutching control
iron-fisted
needing to release
this feeling
then I remind myself
relax

I inhale
focus on my breath
diaphragm filling
lungs inflating
up into exhaling
as worries flow
out between my lips
like soft, airy feathers
cleansing in the air

With each breath
I surrender
a little more
my body softens
with each connection
to a flow of
life energy
I gently fill up
infused with light

I step
into my knowing
a place I've nurtured
once a seedling
reaching for the sun
now a practice
ever deepening
learning to stand
in my divinity

I am but a speck
of light
burning bright
in a symphony of octaves
twirling languidly
within this flowing dance
spreading wide
only to rise

learning to surrender
into
my power
my true self

part shifting-shadows
part eternal light
colliding into oneness
entering into
a flow of love
moment by moment

an act of trust
practicing of faith
as my shadows
taunt and tempt me
into fear,
I chose other
and find strength
to bathe my shadows
in compassion
illuminating them in
pale pink rays
only to turn
to blinding white

this art of surrendering

The House

Carried by the ocean,
I ride the waves,
seafoam green,
tall as towers.
The light, my beacon,
in a storm.
I carry my home,
wherever I go,
Encapsulated and buffered
by outside forces.
I stand alone, rocking, thrown,
almost capsizing,
But my inner strength
is mine,
and mine alone.
I make the waves
my bitch,
I raise my hands
and let go.
I ride the waves

fearlessly,
Knowing,
Knowing,
my inner knowing,
my intrinsic truth,
the truth of who I am.
I am free.
As free as birds that follow
amidst the gray and rolling clouds.
As free as my soul
tethered to the house,
my body, my sacred vessel.
My will is my own.
I shall coast in vastness
of the great waves.
Ever free.

The Truth Seeker

Listen, Dear One
The truth seeker,
seer,
an unblemished vision,
comes to me on the wind.

She sighs
with starstruck eyes,
gently, softly,
showing me the way.

Listen, dear one,
to the voices
singing the song
of all of creation.

To whispers of petals unfolding,
laughter of dancing brooks,
the buzzing of lazy bees,
remaking the world.

To the cry of a newborn,
exhale of the dying,
a circle of existence
in ever-flowing patterns.

She sends her prayers,
on a double rainbow helix,
blessing Gaia after gentle rain,
nourishing all life.

Colors exploding
into chords of vibration,
never-ending spirals,
painting the world anew.

The vision fades
like drifting clouds,
dissipating along the horizon
like a gentle caress of a lover's goodbye.

Leaving me feeling
strangely touched
deep in my sacred heart
with an undeniable knowing.

Her ancient song
dances upon the wind,
a distant sigh upon my skin.
I am here, always, dear one.

Way Show-er

Particles of light,
breathe life
into being.
Spinning through time,
forever,
now,
eternal spirals
of creation.

You are Divine.
Make no mistake,
though we've forgotten
our inheritance.
Activate
the DNA
into a new world.

Power
breathes through you
as you are made
from the same substance

of all of creation.
Lies are our
currency,
waiting for those to listen
born out of suffering.

Give your suffering
a new definition
that spreads
waves of compassion
throughout the world
in form of
sacred prayers.

Uplift
from your place
of darkness,
illuminate the way,
show-er of light.
For our
strength is
born of fire
and contrast.

Let us
lead each other
into a new world
of being.
We are the saviors,
Dear Ones.
coded
deep within

our very
cells.

Hear the call,
answer
ancient songs
being sung in
our name.
In the name of
All that is,
we release that
of which is no longer
for our highest path.

We forge into
darkness,
carving bright,
our light the
beacons for those
who have lost
their way.

Awaken,
Sweet souls,
To your divinity.

Wild Hearts

our beautiful imaginations
want us to know

to shut down thoughts
and let emotions flow

let worlds within bloom
and our hearts unite

illuminating paths
that follow the light

into a journey
powered by the soul

riding a double
helix rainbow

manifesting, cocreating
breathing into now

the crown opens wide
and so love we avow

as divine sovereignty
is ours to claim

and our wild hearts
cannot be tamed

breathe in, lotus style
infusing the heart space

as life force energy flows
bringing us to states of grace

Unity

Sunday school
downstairs
down the stairs

flouncy pink dress
saying prayers
of protection

we sing and color
and play at a park
the hidden park

we sing
Let There Be Peace on Earth
and love our brothers and sisters

and our mothers and fathers
our tribe
in Unity

where Mother Father God,
shines a light
on their children

you too, are Gods, of God
of rainbow colors
and darkness

in starry nights
we love you all
no matter who you are

Welcome
the collection plate
is a wicker basket

folded up checks and
crumpled dollars pay for
piano in the back

but if you can't give
bless the offering
so that it multiplies

All that we have
All that we give
As the form of love

emanating through
the minister's eyes,
the Goddess shining

through,
accompanied by
her beaming smile

205

So Be It
and
So It Is

The Journey of a Writer
Musings

The Dark Night of the Soul

I never imagined that clicking on a random Facebook post early in the pandemic would take me on a journey through the dark night of the soul...writer style. It was a post advertising an online writing workshop. I thought, *'what the heck, why not?'* and decided to join. I desperately needed something during that time to feed my soul and curate joy in my life.

The workshop was nothing as expected. Writing was prompt-based, and other writers, as shown in little zoom boxes, wrote in every style and modality. Together we gathered and wrote our hearts out through invited five to ten-minute activity increments. Sometimes single words were given to write from, other times it was an image or sentence, or a poem. After a specific Invitation's time was up, some volunteered to share what they wrote. I won't lie, the weekly class was intimidating at first, but then our online group's writing time became a beautiful sacred space of creativity and self-growth. And like the rest of the world, I experienced growth in all areas of my life as the world shut down. It felt as if the world was experiencing a mass dark night of the soul, and no one from the collective-consciousness was spared.

And so, I embarked on this weekly-writing journey as the world spun around in a chaotic dance. It felt as though we were all forced to deal with our shadows, as individuals and collectively. Every week I used the writing time as a tool to learn more about myself. *Connecting with one's Self* was another element each workshop focused on, and how to view writing as means for having a conversation with yourself–to learn how to stop writing *for* the outside, and instead how to write *from* the inside. Janna Lopez, the teacher, invited members from the group to stop worrying about how others would view our work, and to focus on what our words had *to tell us*. We slowly learned that when it came to *the process of writing*, there was no right or wrong, no outside audience to cater to, no judgments worthy of adhering to, just a space for expression and freedom, and for whatever discoveries or creations that had arrived through writing.

These teachings were both liberating and uncomfortable at the same time. This invitation-prompt-based approach meant that there were parts of myself that started to speak through the five-minute bursts of writing–parts I'd wanted to keep silent. Parts of myself I forgot even existed started to emerge. The writing, week after week, unearthed a version of me as if I was a mosaic of mystery, un-folding unseen depths of who I was. I found myself discovering and rediscovering pieces of myself. I was invited to face a reality that some of my coping mechanisms I leaned on were things like denial and procrastination. I shoved truths of myself in a box marked "Deal With Later," and wrapped in metaphorical duct tape to contain the pain, or vulnerability, or the honesty, deep within my bones. Until the box busted at the seams.

I began to allow my words to speak to me, inform me, and heal me. I started to write poetry again. I realized that somewhere along the way of adulting, I'd stopped writing poetry. For years, I'd been focused on fictional stories, giving my fictional characters parts of my voice that wanted to be heard. But for me, writing poetry became an entirely other form of creative freedom. It helped me delve into the nitty-gritty of my writing, and I used writing poetry as a tool, or perhaps as a conduit, for my words. I could access and bring forth all that had been festering in the dark places in my soul. Writing poetry helped me see more internal boxes, labeled with things like, "Loss," or "Toxic Relationships." or "That One Soul-Crushing Heartache," or "Hidden Trauma."

All of the writing affirmed that there is such power in using words, especially if they are coming straight from our hearts and souls, with true authenticity. *To be seen.* As the words appeared before me to be acknowledged, parts of my shadow became illuminated. What I found through the weekly guided-writing process was that some of the shiny veneer from my prior writing style fell away. My words became a little darker and more raw, but more vulnerable and honest. With each piece of buried truth that became written into being, a mask fell away, a wall came down. A deeper understanding and compassion for a younger me inspired hope.

I also remembered that there is beauty in darkness. Pain is part of human experience. Some of the hidden truths that eventually came to light helped me find more pieces of my internal mosaic, forever evolving. By writing through kernels of truth, *my truth* as I knew it, I became free. Free to love, or forgive, or to create boundaries.

I look back at the past, and there was this piece I'd written on Medium.com in 2021 called, "I Wonder." The amount of fear and anxiety I had at that time, and see in the piece, blows my mind. I imagine the feelings and experiences in the piece were true for a lot of people. I now wonder what my stress-levels would have been if I didn't have writing to help me through? If I didn't have this beautiful, amazing medium to channel all the creativity and truths I'd held, and had patiently waited, for expression. Where would I have been If I hadn't sought such a supportive writing group and coach?

The truth is, as a writer, I am always changing, learning, evolving. I strive to make my words more authentic and to fall in love with the process as much as the outcome. Perhaps my truth will inspire others to shine theirs, just as I've been inspired by others.

What I learned from unearthing parts of my hidden self, forgotten self, my joyous self through writing, was to offer myself grace. To step out of my comfort zone and share my writing journey. To have the courage to give my silenced words a chance to be heard. To be proud that I feel a little more like myself in my skin.

That fear can be a deterrent or a motivator, for I believe bravery means nothing without that fear. Sometimes accepting the shadow parts of ourselves allows us to experience a new sense of freedom.

This is what the dark night of the soul looked like to me...as a writer.

Ever learning, ever evolving.

And as always, my journey as a writer continues.

Dark Night of the Soul

The dark night of the soul
took its toll
unearthed truths
buried beneath
deep inside
where pain resides
and pulled it through
shattered walls
of carefully constructed lies
so they could no longer hide
emerging from the other side
a little bruised
a little sore
healing from a new
tender core
where light was reborn
making all things new
stretching new limbs that
it grew
where grief and love

reside, collide, imbibe
in our heart's desire
basking in this new
feminine fire
akin to a phoenix rising
soaring to new heights
into this tender flesh
where a dark night of the soul
conspired to make
me whole.

Acknowledgements

This collection of poems and musings has been an act of growth and courage. There are so many people who have been instrumental in the creation and completion of this book. First of all I would like to give a huge thanks to my writing coach, Janna Lopez, and all her students and the ChaChing Writers who have either gone on a similar journey, or encouraged me as we've walked this path separately and collectively. Their encouragement and support means the world to me.

I would also like to acknowledge my Vocal and Medium online support groups, the various publications on Medium, and all the individuals who supported me and each other on this writing journey. You were instrumental in my journey of posting my work online and being seen. We may never meet in person but I probably wouldn't have made it through the Pandemic without your support and connection.

I would like to acknowledge those in my first writer's group, the 'Fiction Junkies' consisting of me, Kesha Ajose Fisher, Ginille Forrest and Kelli Anderson, for your encouragement and honest critiques. Your friendship, support and growth sparked the first flame inside me on this journey of becoming an author.

A shout out to the sisters of my soul, our sacred trinity of contracting in this lifetime to PC our way through life, in love and light. Rebecca Cardoza and

Rachel Stahlman. Your love, support and friendship helped shape me into this beautiful, powerful woman I am becoming. I couldn't imagine living this life without you.

And finally...family. To my husband and son, who might think I'm a bit crazy, but love me anyway. Thank you for letting me be me. To my mother, who has always been my biggest fan.

This book has been a labor of growth and love and all of you helped make it a possibility in one way or another.

About the Author

A.N. Tipton resides in the lush, rainy landscapes of the Pacific Northwest with her husband and son. A lifelong lover of literature, she writes poetry, fiction, and blogs, finding solace and creativity in the written word. Through her blog *The Journey of a Writer* on Medium.com, along with her debut poetry and musings collection *Emerging Through the Shadows*, she explores the complex terrains of spirituality, healing, and human resilience.

Tipton's writing emerges from the intersection of creativity, healing, and vulnerability. Her work has roots in early recognition—her first poem published in the National Library of Poetry as a teenager—and a lifelong commitment to understanding the intricate layers of human experience. Through stream-of-consciousness poetry, intimate musings and fictional short stories, she invites readers into a raw, unfiltered exploration of personal growth, grief, and resilience.

When not writing, you can find her reading a book with a cup of tea. Check out her website at www.antipton.com.

www.ingramcontent.com/pod-product-compliance
Lightning Source LLC
Chambersburg PA
CBHW021236130626
46554CB00004B/1524